T0209316

CULTIVATING
A HEALTHY
VOLUNTEER
TEAM

Practical Steps to Help You Engage, Equip, and Empower Your Volunteers

TRACY BAER, CMP, CFMP

WESTBOW
PRESS®
A DIVISION OF THOMAS NELSON
& ZONDERVAN

This book is a work of non-fiction. Unless otherwise noted, the author and the publisher make no explicit guarantees as to the accuracy of the information contained in this book and in some cases, names of people and places have been altered to protect their privacy.

WestBow Press books may be ordered through booksellers or by contacting:

WestBow Press
A Division of Thomas Nelson & Zondervan
1663 Liberty Drive
Bloomington, IN 47403
www.westbowpress.com
844-714-3454

ISBN: 979-8-3850-0410-2 (sc)
ISBN: 979-8-3850-0411-9 (e)

Library of Congress Control Number: 2023914245

Print information available on the last page.

WestBow Press rev. date: 08/24/2023

Contents

Preface

As the events manager for a large church, I had the pleasure of leading a team of event planners. Our role was to support ministries as they scheduled and executed their events. One specific role of our department was to build and deploy a volunteer team to serve at each event—from preparation to execution to cleanup. Over the years, we had a thriving volunteer team with over five hundred active members, and we supported hundreds of events. Later, I served as the chief operations officer of a nonprofit organization that equipped and educated pastors. Our organization partnered with volunteers to execute our own annual event and multiply the time of our paid staff members as we worked through the planning process. I gained a new set of skills as I learned how to work with a team of volunteers who lived in a different state from both the home office where I was and the state where the event was held. During my time on staff with this organization, the largest pain point the leaders of our community experienced and requested the most resources for assistance with was their volunteers.

Listening to these leaders lament over their struggles inspired me to share the knowledge I gained through many years and different experiences working with successful volunteer teams with others. I had been formulating this book in my mind for years; and after much contemplation, revision, and consultation, here it is. I hope this book provides you with the tools you need to create and maintain a thriving and sustainable volunteer team.

Tracy Baer

Introduction

Many churches, nonprofit organizations, and associations partner with volunteers as an integral part of their daily operations. With generally stricter budgets, these organizations require unpaid assistance to multiply the capacity of paid staff in order to complete their work. Creating a healthy volunteer program where people feel equipped, appreciated, and empowered to perform the tasks needed and who invite others to participate on the team with them can be essential for an organization's survival. This book provides practical information and examples from years of experience and real-life scenarios to help organizations cultivate a healthy team that is sustainable and benefits both the organization and the volunteer.

Several examples in the book reference event volunteers for both in-person and virtual events. The underlying principles, however, are applicable to many other scenarios where volunteer partnership is needed. It also provides examples of leaders who work with volunteers who do not live in their same geographical location and some of the unique dynamics of this relationship.

1

Why Volunteers?

Definition of a Volunteer

Merriam-Webster defines a volunteer as "a person who offers to do something without being forced to or without getting paid to do it."[1] Nonprofit-organization or -association volunteers should also be defined in this way. There are two key takeaways in this statement: (1) do not force people into helping and (2) do not pay them to do it. This does *not* mean an organization does not empower, equip, train, or appreciate a volunteer. These are absolute musts!

---

[1] Merriam-Webster, s.v. "Volunteer," 2023, https://www.merriam-webster.com/dictionary/volunteer.

Value and Impact of Volunteers

Working with volunteers can add value to an organization in ways it may not have ever considered before. Each person contributes their individual life experiences and unique gifts and talents and comes from a different background. As a result, an organization and its staff have an opportunity to learn from the creativity and skills of others. Organizations can then infuse new ideas and perspectives into their daily operations and event planning to connect better with their audience. A volunteer can also contribute a great deal to an organization's marketing strategy, especially for an event. When the volunteers have been empowered with information by the organization, they capture the mission, vision, and values as their own. Volunteers then generate enthusiasm and interest for the organization or event as they interact with their circle of influence and reach others in a way that traditional marketing and advertising cannot.

The impact a team of volunteers has on an organization can be the difference between its success and failure. The to-do list for every organization is lengthy, and most cannot afford to hire enough staff members to accomplish the work. Without enough people to get the work done, mission-critical tasks get prioritized, leaving others unfinished. Do this long enough and the list of uncompleted tasks can overwhelm an organization.

The same principle applies to events. Most nonprofit organizations or associations that execute events partner with volunteers to accomplish their goals. Likewise, the planning checklist for any event is already long; and since 2020, most events have added even more to the checklist with the inclusion of a virtual component. By multiplying the paid staff's time and sharing the work with volunteers, whether on-site or from a remote location, everything can get done without incurring a large amount of additional expenses.

Rewarding Returns

The organization is not the only one who gains from this relationship; the volunteer gains a great deal from participating as well. When serving, a volunteer has the opportunity to pursue an interest, learn something new, develop a skill, or deepen current knowledge. There is intangible value for the volunteer from the experience as well. They can strengthen relationships with other volunteers on the team and with the organization's leaders or meet new people and start new relationships. Some volunteers can even contribute to the team by offering their leadership skills, trade skills, or simply life's wisdom to others. This can bring a sense of fulfillment to a volunteer who is able to impart information to another.* For some who live alone, serving on a team provides them with much-needed human-interaction time. Events often offer one-time serving opportunities for a person to step outside their normal routine or to get connected with an organization in a low- or no-commitment way.

Ultimately, the decision to work with a team of volunteers, pay for temporary workers, or hire staff members is determined by an organization's stakeholders and their goals and objectives. When the stakeholders meet at the onset of a project where volunteers will be involved, agenda items might include budget, number of volunteers needed, timeline for building the team, strategy, and more.

*Tracy's Tip: Alleviate work from the paid staff members and develop volunteer leaders by allowing a volunteer with specialized knowledge or skill to conduct training where applicable. For example, if a volunteer works in communications, have them train other volunteers on reviewing and editing copy for an organization's website or marketing materials.

2

Preparing for the Team

An organization's leaders need to be prepared before engaging a volunteer in a conversation to join the team. Volunteers need a certain amount of information to be able to make an informed decision when determining whether or not to participate on the team. When a leader is prepared with a number of important details ahead of time, it not only helps a volunteer decide if they want to join the team but it also demonstrates a level of value the organization has for its volunteers. It is also evidence of a leader's ability to lead. When a leader is organized and able to answer questions, a volunteer is more likely to feel confident about their decision to serve. Being prepared conveys respect for the relationship with a volunteer by a leader.

Gathering the Details

Before an organization builds its volunteer team, the needs have to be determined. During a meeting of the stakeholders, several decisions need to be made, including, among others, the following:

- What criteria are required of a person to participate on the team?
- What tasks does the organization need to have completed?
- What is the time commitment required to accomplish the tasks?
- What training will be needed to prepare someone to perform the tasks?

Once the organization has established an outline for its needs, a list of specific details can be gathered that will help a volunteer determine if they are able to serve on the team. Details include

- date(s) and time(s) a volunteer will need to commit to,
- a list of tasks a volunteer will be performing,
- type of equipment or supplies that will be provided to a volunteer and ones they may need to bring,

- whether a volunteer needs to dress in a specific way to participate,

- whether a specialized skill is required to perform the tasks, and

- logistical details regarding arrival, parking, and gaining entry to participate.

When building a volunteer team specifically for an event, examples of additional details might include

- location of the event,

- projected attendance,

- audience demographics (i.e., is this an event of rowdy students, or is it a fundraising dinner?),

- schedule of the event,

- how and when training will be provided, and

- whether a volunteer will serve locally on-site or remotely.

As a volunteer team is assembled, constant communication among leaders within an organization is critical for the success of the program. Most decisions leaders make begin a domino effect of changes, and as a result, these can affect the volunteers. It is important for the health of the team that leaders provide updated information to, or schedule regular meetings with, its volunteers to make sure everyone is moving in the same direction together.*

Tracy's Tip: When working with a group of people, some of whom may not live in the same community as the organization, using a project management program is a great tool to keep the team in sync. Members of the team, a list of tasks, files, timelines, and milestones can all be seen and reviewed by everyone in real time.

Designing the Team Structure

Once details are collected, the volunteer structure can be outlined. This includes compiling a list of all tasks and related positions needed. When planning an event, for example, an organization should begin by identifying what tasks need to be accomplished during the planning, execution, closing, and debriefing phases. Once these are identified and refined, roles or positions are developed. An event org chart will begin to take shape through this process, and position descriptions (like job descriptions) start to form. Leaders can be assigned to a group of volunteers, and volunteer team leaders (if applicable) can also be positioned on the team during this process.

In-person and virtual volunteer teams may be structured differently or actually quite similarly depending on the type of event and the tasks that need to be accomplished. The biggest difference between the two is the location of the volunteer while serving—on-site for an in-person event or possibly on-site or remotely for a virtual event.

When a smaller organization wants to partner with only one or two volunteers, creating a whole team structure may seem excessive. The foundational principles of designing a volunteer program and building a team can be applied or modified to fit an organization of any size.

Refer to Resource A in the appendix for a sample menu of volunteer positions.

Number of Volunteers

Once the tasks that need to be performed have been identified, as well as what positions are required to perform them, the number of people needed per position needs to be determined. For example, at an in-person event, if one position is a "room host" and there are ten rooms that need hosting, one person will not be enough. Perhaps one person can monitor two or three rooms so the number of volunteers needed might not be a full ten. Also, if the schedule contains morning and afternoon sessions, the number of volunteers could double if a different team arrives in the afternoon. Leaders of an organization should dedicate some time to thinking through the logistics of an event when determining the number of volunteers needed. This process cannot be omitted without jeopardizing the health of the volunteer team. It is also important for the leaders to consider the demographics of the volunteers serving at the event. A younger demographic of volunteers will most likely be able to work longer hours and take on more physical tasks than an older one, therefore requiring a different number of volunteers.

Team Org Chart

An org chart may seem unnecessary for an unpaid team, but providing one to the volunteers is incredibly helpful. It provides a clear communication structure for the team at every level and can help an organization identify potential areas where a leader could be overwhelmed with too much responsibility or have too many volunteers reporting directly to them. An org chart allows an organization to adjust the team structure before building the team begins. It also helps a volunteer know who their leader is and who else is serving on their team.

When an organization is building a large-scale team, based on the size and scope of the project, it may want to identify and train volunteer team leaders. These volunteer team leaders, like unpaid managers, can oversee a group of volunteers performing tasks in a specific area of the event or project, reducing the workload on the paid staff members. For example, a team of "room hosts" for an in-person event may report to a "volunteer host leader" or "manager" who trains and oversees this group of volunteers. The volunteer leader then reports to an organization's paid staff member. By creating an org chart, everyone knows who reports to whom.

This organization → leader → volunteer team member structure not only helps to keep any single person from feeling overwhelmed with responsibility; it allows for a more personal and relational experience for everyone. It also streamlines the communication pathways for information or changes that need to be relayed to others on the team.

If a small organization is only partnering with one or two volunteers, providing an organization's org chart and indicating how a volunteer fits into that structure will help provide clarity for everyone.

Designing the Team Schedule

Based on the needs of an organization identified through the process of designing the volunteer team structure, a team schedule can then be created. Even if an organization requires the assistance of only one or two volunteers, some parameters need to be set for a volunteer for clarity.

To care for a volunteer well, when creating the schedule, a leader should consider factors such as the following:

- What time of day the schedule starts and ends
- How many consecutive hours an individual would want to serve
- Whether or not a person is serving long enough to need a meal or a break

Where able, having a leader create the schedule in collaboration with a volunteer or team of volunteers will foster relationship building and ensure a more comprehensive schedule. Once an overall team schedule has been determined and the positions and responsibilities identified, individualized volunteer schedules can be created.

If developing a volunteer's schedule for an in-person event, additional event-specific schedule considerations might include

- extra time at the beginning of the schedule if a volunteer needs to park and walk to the event from a remote lot, check in, and receive training;

- time for a volunteer to have a meal or a break if serving for an extended period of time; and
- overlap in volunteer schedules (if a task cannot have a gap in coverage, the incoming volunteer needs to be scheduled to arrive before the outgoing one leaves).

If the volunteer team structure allows for it, a minimum of two volunteers should be scheduled to serve in an area of a large event, or relief volunteers should be scheduled to give volunteers who need a break for a snack or to use the restroom.*

When developing a volunteer's schedule for a virtual event, additional event-specific schedule considerations might include

- calculating the time difference in the schedule if a volunteer's time zone is different than the event time zone and
- in-person volunteer schedules if the virtual event includes a live-hosted, in-studio broadcast for positions like production, catering, and speaker hosts

*Tracy's Tip: Scheduling at least two volunteers to serve together in an area of an event not only gives them someone to talk to, but it also helps to foster relationships among team members. Consider rotating volunteers periodically to allow them to serve with more than one person.

Scheduling by Responsibility or Shift

After the tasks and positions have been established and an overall schedule has been outlined, a decision needs to be made on how to structure a volunteer's schedule. There are two equally effective methods for scheduling volunteers: by *responsibility* or by *shift*. Which one to choose depends on the event's goals and objectives and the experience a leader wants a volunteer to have.

By Responsibility

A schedule created by responsibility means that a volunteer performs a specific role regardless of time. For example, if a volunteer is a "room host" for an in-person event, the volunteer is scheduled to serve every time the room needs hosting. The event schedule will determine the volunteer's schedule for the day and if more than one person will be needed for this role.

For a virtual event, an example would be a volunteer who is moderating a chat feed for a breakout session. Every time that session is scheduled, the volunteer needs to be available to moderate the chat feed. And when a volunteer is scheduled to come to an organization's office to help, an example of this might be a volunteer receptionist. A volunteer serving in this capacity would be needed every time the office was open to greet guests and perform other administrative tasks.

By Shift

A schedule created by shift means that a volunteer performs any task required within a specified amount of time. A leader would determine the amount of time a "shift" is. Typically, a half-day or a four-to-five-hour span of time is considered one shift. This is about the maximum amount of time a volunteer wants to serve at one time before needing a break. A morning shift and an afternoon shift may not be of the same length depending on the event schedule. There may also be three shifts per day if the event schedule starts very early in the morning or ends late in the evening.

When planning a schedule by shift for an in-person event, in a four-hour time span, a volunteer might sell tickets for one hour then help set up and man a coffee station for the next two hours followed by cleanup for the last hour.

A volunteer serving at a virtual event for a four-hour shift might moderate a chat feed for two hours, answer help-center emails for an hour, and monitor a Q&A session chat feed for the last hour. When a volunteer visits an organization's office to serve, a four-hour shift could include a myriad of projects. An office volunteer might edit and print a newsletter for two hours, fold and stuff them into envelopes for another hour, and stamp the envelopes for the final hour.

Position Descriptions

Aside from the length of time they will serve, volunteers want to know what they will be doing. A leader can provide short position descriptions where applicable. This way, a volunteer can determine which position they would prefer to serve in. These descriptions should also include if a volunteer needs to have a special skill or physical ability to perform the task. Since volunteers are not being paid for their service, referring to these as "position" descriptions rather than "job" descriptions helps to differentiate between a paid and unpaid position on the team. An organization may want to consult with its legal counsel to confirm whether or not specific terminology is recommended for their profession or type of project. Position descriptions do not need to be long or all-encompassing; they are designed to align expectations between a volunteer and what an organization is asking of them.

Refer to Resource B in the appendix for sample position descriptions.

TRACY BAER, CMP, CFMP

Preparing the Leader

Besides preparing the necessary event details, another very important aspect of preparing to cultivate a healthy volunteer team is personal preparation by the leader working with the volunteers. As they are preparing, a leader might ask themselves:

- Do I enjoy the work I am doing, or am I feeling burned out?
- Have I set myself up to successfully train and lead others?
- Am I prepared to empower and equip a volunteer for what I am asking of them?
- Does everyone on the team understand how volunteers fit into the plan?

Just like a child takes their emotional cues from their parents in stressful situations, so does a volunteer from their leader. Therefore, a leader needs to be ready. Being prepared may look different for each individual or organization—physically, mentally, emotionally, spiritually, or others; but if a leader is not healthy, the volunteers will feel it. If a leader is feeling overwhelmed, has not prepared to lead, or does not have a margin in their schedule, their stress could manifest in their verbal communication, through body language, or in other interactions with volunteers.

Those who volunteer are usually sacrificing something, like their time, to serve on the team. They have families, friends, full- or part-time jobs (whether inside or outside the home), hobbies, and other responsibilities. They may also be tired and feel overwhelmed in their personal life while they serve. A healthy leader is more capable of reading between the lines and interpreting the body language of a volunteer who might be feeling this way. As the shepherd of the team, a leader may need to have a conversation with a volunteer about how things are going outside of serving with the team.

A leader also wants to lead a team that attracts volunteers to partner with them and shed their blood, sweat, and occasionally tears with them. If a leader is stressed out, they may not have the capacity to create a healthy "work" environment for the volunteers. When a leader is in their own season of overwhelm, they may want to consider stepping back or at the very least having a conversation with their supervisor. Most importantly, leaders and their supervisors should be making sure everyone is taking their vacation time, not working on paid holidays, and scheduling regular activities that refresh and refuel them.

Watching Your Words

It is critical for a leader to monitor how they say what they say. When building the team and reaching out to a volunteer, communication should include clear details and focus heavily on the relationship, but specific words chosen by a leader can impact a volunteer's response positively or negatively. Using words that convey enthusiasm and excitement about being part of a team can evoke a positive reaction from a volunteer.

While being positive and providing the necessary details, a leader cannot disguise information when more challenging work is being asked of a volunteer. Leaders need to be honest with a potential volunteer about the type or amount of tasks that need to be completed. It is also beneficial when a volunteer understands an organization's mission, vision, and values or what the upcoming event is hoping to accomplish. When a volunteer understands the goal and what their contribution is helping to achieve, they are usually more committed to participating on the team than one who does not. People are willing to donate a significant amount of time, talent, and treasure when they feel they are part of something making a difference in the lives of others.

Keeping Your Words

A leader must follow through on what they commit to when working with volunteers. If a leader informs a volunteer they are going to provide training materials by a specific date, it is critical that the deadline is met. If a meeting between a leader and a volunteer is scheduled with a start and end time, it is important that the leader adhere to them. While serving, a volunteer should always be relieved from their shift on time. The volunteer may need to pick up a child from the babysitter or get to their paying job. By following through on the commitments made, a leader is conveying respect for a volunteer and their time. This builds trust between a volunteer and a leader.

Proper expectations also need to be established for a volunteer. If a leader minimizes the work required simply to fill a position with a warm body, a volunteer arriving to perform the tasks may not be adequately prepared. Some volunteers need time to mentally prepare for certain tasks, others may not possess the required skills to perform the task, and still, others may find themselves not dressed appropriately. A volunteer should not be caught off guard when they arrive to serve. When this happens, a volunteer can lose confidence in a leader and may have doubts about serving again.

A leader can cultivate a healthy volunteer team simply by doing what they say they will do. Building trust, gaining the confidence of the volunteers, earning their respect, and conveying how much a leader cares for their well-being is often done without saying a word. A volunteer is more likely to serve again and invite others to serve with them if they trust and respect the leaders they serve with.

3

Building the Team

Screening the Team

When a leader lives in the same community as the volunteers, it is easier to interact with and get to know people. Relationships can be built as a natural side effect of being in proximity to each other. Over the course of time, a leader may learn about a volunteer's passions, skills, or talents; what they do for a living; information about their family; and more. This information is not gained through an interview but can be gleaned when waiting for kids at the bus stop, standing in line at the grocery store, or before yoga class. Then when the time comes to build a volunteer team, a leader can make a personal invitation to a volunteer because they are known by them. Not only that, but a volunteer can be assigned a position they are suited for because a leader understands what they are capable of. The team can be built on relationships.

When volunteers serving on a team live in a different geographical location from a leader, it changes the way the team is assembled. An example of this is an organization hosting an event in a different state from its home office and is partnering with local volunteers in the state where the event is being held. In this case, a leader may not know anyone personally. Potential volunteers may be related to the venue and not the event or organization. People may have been invited to serve by another volunteer or a person may have stumbled onto the organization's website, and neither of these groups of people know anything about the event, the organization, or the leaders.

Regardless of how familiar a leader is with potential volunteers, each person should be screened before being placed on the team. This can be done by having every volunteer complete an application.* It allows a leader to ask specific questions and keeps the intake process consistent for everyone. Then when assembling the team, a leader can review answers to questions to better understand who a volunteer is and can assign them to a position that suits them. It also allows a leader to gather information efficiently, such as contact information, emergency contact, volunteer availability, and more. This could be the most valuable tool for a leader assembling a volunteer team from a remote location. The leader can begin learning about the volunteers and their skills or passions before they meet. This will ultimately lead to a better experience for everyone as the relationships evolve.

Refer to Resource C in the appendix for sample questions for an application.

Information collected using an application is dictated by what needs to be accomplished by and for the volunteer team. If a volunteer will be coming to the organization's office to help transcribe meeting notes, questions may be specifically designed to determine a volunteer's typing skills. If a volunteer is serving remotely from their home for a virtual event, questions may be related to a volunteer's ability to use a computer or a broadcast platform. If a volunteer is serving on-site at an in-person event and the organization is providing housing accommodations for the volunteers, questions should help determine roommate assignments. If unique skills are required for a position, a leader will want to screen out volunteers who do not qualify. For example, if a task is running a projector for a PowerPoint presentation and a volunteer is not comfortable with technology in general, this person should not be selected for the role. Without asking the proper questions during the application process, the experience for the leader and the volunteer could be less than ideal.

When a leader does not have a personal relationship with a volunteer, it is impossible for a leader to know their passions and preferences. If a person serves best "behind the scenes" and not "on the front lines," this volunteer would thrive in a position that sits in the office and staples information packets together but would want to quit if assigned as a door greeter.

An application is only one tool a leader can use to screen volunteers. A leader can also schedule a personal conversation or interview, similar to a job interview, with a potential volunteer. This gives a leader an opportunity to screen for cues that cannot be gleaned from a sterile application. Reading body language, discerning familiarity with the language needed to perform the task, and the ability to ask clarifying questions are benefits to a leader when meeting a volunteer face-to-face, even if over a video platform. And depending on the organization, event, tasks, or audience a volunteer will be interacting with, it is appropriate to ask for and check personal or professional references. Volunteers working with children or handling money should also submit to a background check.

Tracy's Tip: If a leader uses an application to assign positions to volunteers they are not personally familiar with, as volunteers are serving, the leader should make observations of what is going well and what is not. It is possible that questions on the application need to be modified or a volunteer may have been placed in a position they were not suited for. A leader can also note if certain volunteers excel in specific areas or tasks. This information will be helpful when assigning volunteers to future roles and allow for improvements to the process.

Invite, Don't Recruit

Nobody wants to be recruited, army volunteered, or voluntold. Remember *Merriam-Webster*'s definition of volunteering, "without being forced to"? People want to be invited to something fun like a party. Everyone wants to be invited to the movies or coffee with a friend. These invitations make a person feel included, valued, and loved. It is no different for a group of people who are willing to share their time, talent, and sometimes treasure to serve on a volunteer team.

When a leader invites someone to be part of a volunteer team, they can feel a sense of belonging from the very beginning. When making a personal connection, a leader can invite a volunteer to be part of the journey and share the upcoming opportunity with them. A leader can create the same desire and attraction as an invitation for coffee. While sharing their excitement, a leader should always set the proper expectations about what they are asking of a volunteer and not mix enthusiasm with flattery. Personal invitations by a leader or from another volunteer already serving on the team are the most successful ways to cultivate the growth of a volunteer team.

Don't Act Desperate

Leaders building a volunteer team should not use language that implies they are desperate for help. They must not beg or plead for a volunteer to participate on the team. When a leader portrays themselves as overwhelmed and stressed out to a potential volunteer, especially if this person is new to the team, it could deter or discourage them from participating. This behavior sends the message to a potential volunteer that a leader might not be organized, does not communicate well, is not a strong leader, or is not capable of overseeing a team. This can breed a lack of confidence in a leader or organization by a volunteer. A leader may be frazzled on occasion, but when those days happen, a wise leader would choose a different day to reach out to potential volunteers. To have a healthy team, potential volunteers need to trust the one leading the team from the first interaction to the last. Volunteers need reassurance they are serving on a winning team.

Matching People and Positions

Whether screening volunteers using an application or a leader has a personal relationship with a volunteer, a leader should take time to understand each person's gifts, talents, and personality. A leader needs to do their due diligence to fit the right person to the right position. Questions a leader might want to know about a potential volunteer include the following:

- Is the volunteer an introvert or an extrovert?
- What is the person physically able to do?
- Does the person have unique skills or education?
- What life experiences does the person have?
- How old is the person?
- What is the person's availability?
- Have I had experience with this person's past performance?

There is nothing worse for both a leader and a volunteer than having a volunteer serve in a position that is diabolically opposed to their inherent nature. The experience will be miserable for the volunteer who is serving outside of their skillset, and it can negatively affect other volunteers' experience. It can affect the organization as well. For example, if an event volunteer serving on the tech team is responsible for recording a speaker's session but is uncomfortable with audiovisual equipment or is an introvert, the recording may not be captured. This volunteer may be too nervous to push the buttons for fear they will get it wrong, or they may be too shy to enter a crowded room of people. Now the organization has missed the opportunity to record the speaker while on-site.

For those organizations implementing a volunteer program for the first time or if it is a leader's first year building a team, this first one will be the most challenging. A leader should anticipate there will be an occasional mismatch between a volunteer and a task or position. Where possible, a leader might want to make changes on the fly during an in-person event and swap volunteers around. If a volunteer is serving at an organization's office and this happens, a leader might offer additional training or redeploy a volunteer to a different department. Situations like these provide a leader with opportunities to develop their skills and grow in their ability to cultivate a healthy volunteer team.

Setting Proper Expectations

When inviting a volunteer to serve in a specific position, a leader should ensure the volunteer understands the time commitment and responsibilities they are agreeing to. The relationship between a leader and a volunteer can quickly become strained when there are mismatched expectations. Providing written documentation that outlines detailed expectations of both the volunteer and the leader or organization will help reduce any confusion. Also, by providing written documentation, the information can be recalled or referenced as needed.

Volunteer Handbook

Creating and distributing a volunteer handbook is a great asset a leader can use for sharing expectations and information with volunteers. It can reduce the number of emails sent to the volunteer team and save a leader a significant amount of time. The handbook can serve as the single location for the critical details a volunteer will need. A handbook can also include more detailed information or instructions, such as screenshots, diagrams, infographics, or images. When used well, a handbook will cut down on a volunteer's need to save emails, bookmark links, or remember which document contained what information. A helpful volunteer handbook will include practical information, such as venue details, org chart, emergency information, basic protocols, and more. A great handbook will include information from every department that interacts with the volunteer team, contain some history or context for the serving opportunity or event, and reinforce the mission, vision, and values of the organization.

Refer to Resource D in the appendix for a sample handbook table of contents.

Volunteer Agreement

Having a volunteer sign an agreement is helpful for a couple of reasons. First, it is a great way to summarize and provide clarity around what is being asked of a volunteer and what a volunteer can expect from a leader or organization in return. The agreement should define the responsibilities or tasks a volunteer agreed to perform; who the volunteer reports to; the date, time, and length of time a volunteer will serve; and anything else the leader would need to hold a volunteer accountable for. Likewise, if an organization is responsible to a volunteer for anything while they serve such as providing meals and complimentary event tickets or reimbursing expenses like flights or hotel costs, these should also be detailed clearly in the agreement.

Second, the physical act of signing an agreement elevates the level of commitment by a volunteer. Another reason an organization might need to have an agreement is to communicate required disclaimers or waivers that a volunteer needs to acknowledge in order to serve. An organization may want to consult with their legal counsel to see if these types of documents or clauses are required for their profession or type of project.

Expecting the Team

When a volunteer arrives, a leader should make them feel as if they were expected: the table is set, dinner is in the oven, and the door is open. Leaders who are still running around gathering supplies or are late to meet a volunteer start the volunteer's experience off in a negative way. Being ready when a volunteer arrives conveys respect for the volunteer and their time and that the leader cares about their relationship.

When working with volunteers during an in-person event, for example, a leader might want to consider reserving a dedicated location where volunteers can check in or take a break. Based on space and budget, this "volunteer central" room can be a place where volunteers not only check in but also receive last-minute instructions, pick up a copy of a venue map or training materials, grab a refreshment, or sit down when they need to rest. Meals for the volunteers could be served in this room as well. Having this room available gives a volunteer space away from the hustle and bustle of an event. If event plans change, as they often do, communication can be initiated and distributed from this room to volunteers. Additionally, if a volunteer has completed a task early, they can come to this room and find a leader who can reassign them. Recommendations for this room include

- a way to track whether or not a volunteer has checked in;
- identification to provide a volunteer, such as a name tag, lanyard, or T-shirt;
- copies of important documents for a volunteer like a venue map, training materials, or schedule; and
- refreshments like coffee, water, and snacks (preferably something "grab 'n' go").

Ideally, an organization would staff this room with a room host. This can be one of the volunteer positions created when building the team structure. This conveys another level of preparedness by a leader for the volunteers. Having a person or two in this room at all times streamlines communication (one place for everyone to go) and makes check-in easy for a volunteer no matter what time they arrive. Also, by always staffing this room, volunteers can leave purses, backpacks, coats, or any other items they would prefer not to carry on them while they serve. When using radios to communicate, a room host can notify a leader when their volunteers arrive so the leader is prepared to receive them.

An example of a leader expecting a volunteer who is serving at a virtual event might include a leader performing a pre-event technology test to ensure a volunteer's equipment is functioning properly. They may walk through powering up the volunteer's computer, connecting to the event site, checking internet speed, and testing the volunteer's microphone. The leader may also confirm the volunteer has a current event schedule, training documents, and emergency contact information of the leader should they have questions during the event. If a volunteer is serving at an organization's office, a leader should be there before the volunteer arrives. If space and budget allow, a leader can prepare a designated space or workstation where a volunteer can perform their tasks while on-site. Being prepared like this helps make a volunteer feel like the leader was expecting them.

4

Readying the Team

Informing Them

It is important that a leader stays in regular communication with the volunteers. This can be done in a variety of ways. If a leader and volunteer live in the same community, they can meet for coffee or lunch. When a leader lives in proximity to the volunteers, it is easier to schedule an in-person training, appreciation gathering, or informational meeting with a larger group of volunteers all at once. If a leader lives in a different state or some other remote location from the volunteers they serve with, a leader may opt to schedule videoconference calls with volunteers either one-on-one or in groups. The reason for these interactions is not only to convey information but also to continue to build relationships between a leader and the volunteers.

The type of information and how much to share depends on the organization, event, leader, and what needs to be accomplished. Some organizations worry that providing too much information to a volunteer can lead to too many questions. Others find that having informed volunteers is critical to their success, and when a volunteer asks a question, it lets a leader know the volunteers are reading the materials and taking their responsibilities seriously. Good questions also help identify bits of information that may have been overlooked in the original communication, which should be added to future ones.

When providing information to a volunteer, a leader should use a simple format like bullet point emails or short video recordings. A leader can then attach more detailed documents, such as training materials or maps that can be printed and referenced by a volunteer. When crafting an email, the most essential information should be prioritized at the top. By doing this, if a volunteer only scans the email, they will most likely catch the most important points. When communication is too long, people tend to skim or skip it and miss vital details.

In the days leading up to serving, volunteers expect a lengthier "know-before-you-go" communication with last-minute details from a leader. While still focusing on the relationship, these communications need to be clear and articulate. This is not the time a leader should develop their creative writing skills.

Be Specific

When a leader is relaying information to a volunteer, it is important to include relevant details. For example, when providing arrival information to a volunteer serving at an in-person event, it is helpful to provide more than just the arrival time. In addition to the time, specific details such as venue address, which room a volunteer checks into, who the volunteer checks in with, and where to park will be critical. If a leader wants to go above and beyond, they can also inform a volunteer about any construction in the area or if they should eat a meal before they arrive.

For a team of volunteers serving in a remote location separate from a leader, a leader might want to communicate details such as the date and time to be logged into their computer, what website or link to log into, the type of device a volunteer should use, and what internet speed is required. A leader may also want to provide a volunteer with information, such as which internet browser to use and how to troubleshoot common audio or video issues. When a leader is working with a volunteer who is coming to the organization's office to serve, details a leader may want to share are similar to those for an in-person event: where a volunteer should park, which door of the building to enter, and what to wear. Some volunteers get nervous before serving, and providing them with plenty of details can reassure them.

Training Them

Not every volunteer performs the same task in the exact same way. A leader should provide training for any task that needs to be done with consistency and accuracy. If a leader really wants a task done in a specific way, they can provide training materials in not only written format but also using images, screenshots, or diagrams. When a leader provides instructions using different mediums, the chances of the volunteers performing a task correctly and consistently increase. When and what type of training a leader should provide depends on the organization, leader, volunteers, and timeline as well as the complexity of the tasks that need to be accomplished.

If time allows, it is beneficial when training materials can be sent to a volunteer prior to when they are scheduled to serve.

This allows a volunteer additional time when needed to review or process the materials at their own pace. A leader can also include links to external references, such as equipment manuals and industry expert how-to videos. If the task to be performed by a volunteer includes preparing banquet tables at an event, for example, a leader can set up one table as a sample, take a picture, and include the picture in the training materials. This way, a volunteer can replicate the setup without direct supervision.

When a volunteer team consists of people who are not familiar with one another or who serve on different days, to help cultivate a healthy team, it is highly recommended that a leader gather the entire team from time to time. Based on time and budget including a meal or dessert with this gathering is a good way to entice volunteers to show up. When a leader gathers volunteers in this manner, it not only allows for hands-on training and face-to-face interactions but also provides space for relationship building among the team. Additionally, it can be a time to introduce organizational staff members or volunteer team leaders to the entire team at once.

If a leader works with a remote team of volunteers, this type of gathering can still be done using a video platform. The training may need to be modified for a virtual setting, but with the technology available, much interaction and relationship building can still take place between volunteers and leaders.

On-the-job training is another option. Pairing a new volunteer with a trained one encourages volunteers to work together and empowers the trained volunteer with a leadership role. Often, on-the-job training works best for tasks such as digital payment systems for merchandise or ticket sales, for example, as the equipment for these positions is usually limited by quantity and location.

Write It Down

Providing volunteers with written instructions or procedures is the best way to set them up for success. Not only does it help ensure that different volunteers will perform the same task in the same manner more consistently and accurately, but it also allows a volunteer to reference the information anytime they want to. Written information also helps reduce confusion or conflict among volunteers. It is incredibly important that all volunteers receive the same information whether it is shared via a shared document, an email, or in-person training materials. A leader needs to ensure that the information is finalized before being distributed and that only one version of training materials exists for a single task. This can be accomplished by sending a link where instructions can only be viewed ahead of the time a volunteer will be performing the task. This way, the information is always current and always the only one available to volunteers. A leader should also consider the experience and competency levels of the volunteers when determining what and how training materials are communicated.

Without written materials, each individual volunteer is left to interpret how to perform certain tasks through their own experiences and filters. This can cause confusion and potential conflict among members of the team. Confusion can cause frustration or disagreements between volunteers. This behavior can create a negative experience for volunteers and leaders and, if during an event, perhaps the audience as well. It can even ultimately affect the goals and objectives that an organization is trying to achieve. To continue to cultivate a healthy volunteer team, a leader needs to provide clear written materials where possible.

Welcoming Them

As well as expecting a volunteer when they arrive, a leader needs to welcome them. A welcoming atmosphere can be created by a leader simply by smiling and acknowledging a volunteer when they arrive. Whenever possible, a leader should greet each volunteer by name. This immediately sends the message to a volunteer that a leader knows and sees them. As mentioned before, if the budget and space allow, having a designated room where a volunteer can check in to serve at an in-person event or creating a workspace in an office setting that is dedicated to a volunteer welcomes them into a space and into a relationship with a leader or organization.

As a bonus, a leader might consider something to surprise and delight a volunteer when they arrive, such as a welcome bag for someone serving for the first time. The bag could contain basics like a name tag, lanyard, and training materials and also fun items, like logo apparel, snacks, or a coffee shop gift card. To really make a volunteer feel welcome, a leader can include a note with a welcome message from the organization.

When leading a virtual volunteer team, making a volunteer feel welcome could be a welcome text or email to a volunteer on the morning of the event. A welcome email could include a personal note from a leader, an event schedule, and an electronic gift card to an online store. When welcoming a volunteer who is arriving at the organization's office to serve, a leader must be available to meet the volunteer when they arrive and escort them to their workstation. Along the way, the leader can introduce the volunteer to others working around them, give them a tour of the space, and provide helpful information before they begin.

5

Leading the Team

Lending a Hand

Volunteers want to serve with leaders who are competent and professional. They also want to know that a leader will step in and lend a hand if needed. It sets a great example for the team when a leader can identify a need, determine what has to happen next, and when necessary, roll up their sleeves to get the job done. When a leader serves alongside a volunteer, it provides an opportunity for relationship building and gives them a chance to learn something about one another. A leader can also take advantage of this time to coach a volunteer in different areas such as skill, educate them on a subject, or help them to adjust to being on the team. When volunteers see a leader investing in the team, it continues to build the trust and respect a volunteer has for a leader.

Conversely, a leader can quickly lose credibility in the eyes of a volunteer when they appear to be arrogant or unwilling to help out. Leaders who do not interact with the volunteers while they serve can earn a reputation for being unfriendly. If this type of negative opinion of a leader starts to circulate among the volunteer team, a leader could find themselves serving alone. Even if a leader delegates the work to someone else, the mere fact that they recognize that work needs to be done and find a solution for the issue sends the message to a volunteer that the leader is on their side.

Keeping It Together

As stated before, a volunteer will take their emotional cues from their leader much like a child does from its parent. It is critical that a leader maintains their professional and controlled demeanor regardless of what type of challenges arise. Volunteers want to know their leader is capable of leading them. The best opportunity a leader has to show the team their qualifications is when put to the test. It is important that a leader stays calm under pressure, looks people in the eye, considers all the facts, and makes a decision.

If a leader begins to panic or run around frantically, volunteers will sense that something may be wrong. This uneasiness trickles throughout a volunteer team, causing some to become uncertain of their role in the issue, question their decision to serve, or shake their faith in a leader. In extreme cases, some volunteers may opt to just leave and go home to avoid getting involved.

Volunteers are attracted to, and will follow, a leader who can solve problems, is not afraid to make decisions, provides them with guidance and encouragement, and can keep it together when a challenge hits them in the face. Leaders like this are not only able to cultivate healthy volunteer teams but grow them as well.

Making Connections

It is not only important for a leader to be available and prioritize time to talk with volunteers while they serve but also to foster and facilitate conversations between volunteers. A leader should make introductions when volunteers are serving together who do not know one another. A leader can provide a tidbit of information that two people have in common during the introduction when the leader has a personal relationship with the people on their team. Some volunteers are introverted or shy and may need encouragement from a leader to start a conversation with someone else. This example by a leader of desiring to connect with others can permeate a volunteer team and inspire others to reach out and make introductions on their own.

Organizations that introduce new volunteers to the team might want to incorporate a mentor-style program. When using this program, a leader matches a new volunteer with a seasoned volunteer for a period of time. A new volunteer can ask questions of the seasoned one, and the seasoned volunteer can provide "insider information" to the new one, information the seasoned volunteer may have learned while serving with the team that is not in any training materials. A seasoned volunteer can also facilitate introductions to others on the team as they serve or train together.

Making sure that everyone on the team is wearing a name tag will help the entire team learn one another's names and reduce awkward moments during conversations when volunteers know they have been introduced to one another but someone has forgotten a name.

Paying Attention

Observing Them

While volunteers are serving, a leader should always monitor the volunteers: what they are doing, how they are doing it, and what is happening around them. Besides the fact that the leader is responsible for the team, a leader should always be looking for volunteers to raise up, someone who demonstrates leadership qualities, takes ownership of their role, assumes additional responsibilities, or solves problems. Volunteers like this may be good candidates for future team leaders or organizational staff members.

Another reason a leader should keep an eye on the volunteers is that some are afraid or unwilling to ask for help. A volunteer might be feeling overwhelmed by the tasks they are performing or they are wearing out and need a break. A leader can observe this in the body language of the volunteer when they are paying attention. If noticed, the leader can either step in and lend a hand or provide additional volunteer support even if the volunteer has not spoken up.

Conversely, it is possible that a particular area of an event or position on the team is overstaffed and volunteers are standing around looking bored. A leader who is watching the volunteers could redeploy some to other areas where they may be more useful or relieve some to go home.

Occasionally, there will be a volunteer on the team who has a behavior issue affecting those around them that needs to be addressed by the leader. This volunteer may be prone to gossip or is dissatisfied with some aspect of their position, the tasks, a leader, or the organization. This volunteer can poison those around them quickly if left unchecked. A watchful leader can intervene quickly and have a conversation with the volunteer to determine their ability to continue to serve as well as their desire to remain on the team.

Listening to Them

When speaking with volunteers while they serve, a leader needs to really listen to what they have to say. It is important for a leader to learn the volunteers' names, what their hobbies are, and what special or unique gifts or talents they have. This is not only important for building relationships with the volunteers, but it will also help the leader when assigning a volunteer to a specific position in the future if they choose to serve again. Plus, volunteers have a great deal to contribute to the program, event, or organization.

Besides having a casual conversation with a volunteer, there are intentional ways a leader can collect helpful information from them. One way would be to send each volunteer a post-serve survey. A leader can ask specific questions about a volunteer's serving experience, their interactions with leaders they reported to, or other volunteer-program-specific questions. These are helpful to a leader when reviewing, refining, and improving the volunteer program. Volunteer feedback is a critical piece of the puzzle when cultivating a healthy volunteer team.

A leader can also ask a volunteer general questions about observations made while they served, especially during an in-person event, for example. These are helpful to an organization as they review the goals and objectives of the event as a whole. A leader cannot always be everywhere, and volunteers can provide vital information and insight. Allowing a volunteer to share their experience also honors the commitment a volunteer made to the organization by serving.

Another way a leader can listen to a volunteer is to schedule either a team debrief meeting with the whole team or select volunteers from the team or schedule one-on-one interviews with specific volunteers. The same questions asked on a post-serve survey can be used for these meetings as well. The results are the same: a leader will have the chance to hear from the volunteers who served and learn from them.

One important question a leader should ask a volunteer after they serve is, "Would you serve with this organization or leader again?" The answer to this question will tell a leader how the volunteer's experience went overall. If the answer is no, then a leader has work to do. There is room for improvement in the program in some capacity. If this is the case, it will be important for a leader to ask follow-up questions to gain clarity. If the answer is yes, a leader should feel pretty good about the health of the volunteer team and the program.

Another question a leader might ask is, "Would you invite a friend or family member to serve with you next time?" If a volunteer had a positive enough experience to want to share it with a friend or family member, a leader can feel confident they are growing and maintaining a healthy volunteer team.

Refer to Resource E in the appendix for sample questions to ask a volunteer after they serve.

Thanking Them

A leader absolutely cannot overlook this step. It is probably the most important one when cultivating a healthy volunteer team. Working with a volunteer team is not just about getting tasks accomplished; it is about relationships; the relationship a volunteer has with a leader, the relationship a volunteer has with the tasks they are performing, and the relationship a volunteer has with other volunteers. Volunteers want to serve on a team where they feel appreciated versus a team where they may feel taken advantage of. A leader must thank a volunteer for sharing their time, talent, or treasure; acknowledge their contribution; and appreciate their service. Where possible, anytime a leader can thank a volunteer publicly or in front of the audience they served, they should. This reinforces to the audience that unpaid volunteers helped make their program possible, honors the volunteers, and reminds the volunteers who they ultimately served.

There are infinite ways a leader can thank a volunteer.* The most limiting factors are budget, time, or space. A leader can be as creative and generous as the organization allows. The point is not what the thank-you is but that the thank-you recognizes the relationship a leader or organization has with the volunteers and the commitment they made. A volunteer is more likely to participate with the team again if they felt seen and appreciated by the leader they served with.

*Tracy's Tip: I recommend a leader send each volunteer on their team a handwritten thank-you card. Everyone loves to receive one, and it expresses to a volunteer that a leader thought about them long enough to write them a note.

6

Shepherding the Team

Keeping Watch

Over time, a leader will have the opportunity to work with a variety of volunteer personalities. Most volunteers are eager to serve and are incredibly helpful. A volunteer willingly partners with an organization to further their mission, save an organization money in their budget, and be part of something bigger than themselves. There are four prominent personalities that seem to emerge on every large team that a leader needs to understand how to shepherd to ensure everyone is a contributing member of the team. If not handled properly, these volunteers could be a distraction and prevent other volunteers, and themselves, from accomplishing the tasks they are responsible for.

The Tried and True

These are generally rock-star volunteers. They partner with an organization on a regular basis and are familiar with leaders on the team. A volunteer like this shows up early and stays late, will do anything asked of them, and does it with a smile. This type of volunteer has an influence on the team and can be mentored and developed to be a volunteer team leader. This would be the perfect volunteer to ask to onboard a new volunteer or to create and lead a training program for the team. A leader should watch for an entitled attitude from a volunteer like this. Whether intentional or not, occasionally, a longtime volunteer with a lot of organizational knowledge can feel superior to others if not shepherded well. This does not happen with many tried and true volunteers but is something a leader should be mindful of.

The Talker

This volunteer may be a great asset to the team. They can be very engaging, helpful volunteers and contribute a great deal to an organization. However, if not monitored, they may talk to another volunteer all day. If not shepherded appropriately, a volunteer with a chatty tendency can monopolize another volunteer who is either too kind to interrupt or does not know how to get out of the conversation. Potentially, neither volunteer will accomplish the tasks they are responsible for because they are too busy talking. Also, the volunteer who was captured by a talkative one may have a limited or unfavorable experience serving because of this encounter and may not want to return to serve on the team again.

A leader who encounters a volunteer who loves to talk to others simply needs to be aware of them, who they are serving alongside, and whether or not their tasks are getting done. It is possible a leader will need to intervene and refocus a talkative volunteer.

The Complainer

Any leader who has worked with volunteers for any length of time has unfortunately encountered a complaining one. This volunteer may complain to a leader about something specific or they may just grumble to those serving around them. If this volunteer has a valid concern, a leader should take time to listen to them and address it. However, when this volunteer complains for complaining's sake, a leader needs to protect the team.

If the volunteer wants to discuss a specific problem, a leader can encourage this volunteer to also be part of the solution. The volunteer may decide that being part of the solution is too much work or that the specific issue is actually fine the way it is and let it go. If a volunteer is sharing their negativity with others on the team, however, it may cause confusion, dissension, or fractured relationships between members or members and leaders. A volunteer with this personality needs to be attended to directly and swiftly. A conversation may reveal a personal issue the volunteer needs to deal with, and a leader can provide the next steps for them or they may need to be asked to step away from the team for some time. This category of volunteers is not always toxic. They can be good contributors to the team; however, they do need careful monitoring.

The Melancholy

A volunteer of this nature might be a pleasant enough person to be around on occasion. Unfortunately, this type of volunteer usually has something going on in their life that is weighing heavily on them, and they are looking for someone to share it with. They might be lonely and want to share their life's story with the next listening ear. What they may need is a counselor. What they end up doing is verbally vomiting their issues on volunteers serving around them. It is also possible that this category of volunteer is addicted to the attention they receive when others feel compassion for their stories.* If a depressive volunteer is not attended to, and quickly, an unsuspecting volunteer can have hours of their time consumed by this person. A leader may also need some assistance when working with this category of volunteer. A volunteer in this state of mind may not be thinking clearly, may not listen to or hear what a leader is saying to them, or misunderstand or misinterpret what is being said. When speaking with a volunteer like this, having a second leader or an organization's staff member included is wise. Shepherding this type of volunteer can take a lot of patience and time.

*Tracy's Tip: I have worked with a volunteer who was addicted to attention. Ultimately, I had to ask them to refrain from participating on the team so as not to take focus away from the purpose of their service.

7

Improving the Team

Developing Them

An organization working with volunteers should include leadership development as part of the overall volunteer program. This outlines the process for a leader to invite a volunteer into a deeper relationship with an organization. It provides the framework around engaging, screening, training, and promoting a volunteer on the team. Through this system, a leader can discover and develop a volunteer's gifts and talents and appropriately incorporate a volunteer into a leadership position. A leader should always be looking for volunteers who can partner with them and learn the detailed intricacies of their position. It is important for the health of the leader, the strength of the volunteer team, and the longevity of an organization to have volunteers with a higher level of institutional knowledge. If something were to happen to a leader, a highly trained volunteer leader could step in and cover their responsibilities.

A leadership development program establishes the steps an organization feels a volunteer needs to take, or milestones a volunteer needs to pass, to be a successful leader on the team. This process will look different for each organization based on its goals and objectives, mission, vision, values, and types of positions it hopes to fill using volunteer leaders. Developing a volunteer through the steps to leadership will take dedication and time and should be a side-by-side process with a leader. Hands-on learning is invaluable to most volunteers, and building a relationship with a rising volunteer leader is critical for their success within an organization. It is also important for the health of the program that all stakeholders in the organization are invested in developing volunteer leaders.

Pruning Them

Occasionally, there will be a volunteer who may not be suited to continue to serve with an organization. It happens from time to time that a leader needs to ask a volunteer to leave the team. It is important for the health and future of the team that a leader has a conversation with any volunteer who is disruptive to the team in any way. A leader should listen to the volunteer, seek understanding, explain what behavior was observed, and strive for reconciliation where possible. By seeking to fully understand a situation, a leader can make the best decision possible concerning the volunteer's future on the team. If appropriate, a leader may also recommend the volunteer explore professional or pastoral guidance. Sometimes it is necessary for a leader to simply end the relationship with a particular volunteer.

A situation requiring a leader to ask a volunteer to step away from the team is not always the result of a negative experience. Occasionally, a volunteer will overcommit themselves either in serving, working, or a combination of both. These volunteers often will not excuse themselves from serving. An observant leader who has a relationship with their volunteers may take notice and bring what they observe to the volunteer's attention. A leader might recommend the volunteer step away for a season before an adverse life situation occurs. Cultivating a healthy volunteer team can sometimes include asking someone to leave the team for their good or the good of the team as a whole.

Retaining Them

Not only do organizations want to continually add new volunteers to their teams but retain faithful ones who understand their mission and act as advocates for the organization as well. Tenured volunteers are precious and add tremendous value to a team. Volunteers appreciate and will stay connected to a team when they feel heard, appreciated, equipped, and empowered. They remain with an organization when its leaders have gained their trust and respect and have taken the time to invest in relationships with their volunteers.

Consistent communication between a leader and the volunteers is important for retention. A leader needs to be intentional about scheduling time for conversations with members of the volunteer team, especially key volunteer leaders. Prioritizing these check-ins conveys to a volunteer that a leader values them. Seeking a volunteer's opinion on a subject, listening to their feedback, implementing their suggestions, and responding to their concerns are ways a leader can invest in their relationship with a volunteer. It is also mission-critical that communication between a leader and a volunteer happens in seasons when a volunteer is not actively serving. If a leader only reaches out to a volunteer when they are asking them to serve, a volunteer may feel that the only reason for the relationship is to get something from them.

Another important aspect of retaining volunteers is having a leader facilitate community among volunteers on the team. A leader should be intentional about connecting volunteers to one another, making introductions, sharing information where appropriate, and pairing volunteers together when serving or training. Offering the volunteers a system for communicating with one another in between serving opportunities continues to keep relationships alive and encourages volunteer retention. This can be done using an app or through a closed social media group. By cultivating this sense of belonging among volunteers on the team, they have a deeper connection with one another, the leaders, and the organization and are more likely to stay active on the team.

Conclusion

Cultivating means "to develop or improve by education or training; improve the growth by labor and attention."[22] Cultivating a healthy volunteer team takes an investment of time by leaders; it does not just happen. Organizations with a history of successfully engaging and retaining volunteers have prioritized relationships with the volunteers over the reason why they need volunteers in the first place. These organizations intentionally educate and empower volunteers, develop volunteers into leaders, and provide an environment where volunteers can thrive. It is important to maintain constant

---

[2] Merriam-Webster, s.v., "Cultivate," 2023, https://www.merriam-webster.com/dictionary/cultivate.

communication with volunteers, routinely seek their feedback, and allow for improvements to the volunteer program.

Committed volunteers can multiply a paid staff's precious time and protect an organization's budget. Volunteers who have internalized an organization's mission, vision, and values are also great advocates for it. They can expand an organization's reach exponentially when sharing with others in their circle of influence and contribute to an organization realizing its goals. Volunteers also grow the team by inviting other volunteers to participate with them.

By implementing some of the practices in this book, an organization can increase the number of volunteers on their teams, deepen relationships with volunteers, and retain quality volunteers longer. With patience, dedication, attention, sun, and a little water, any organization can cultivate a healthy volunteer team.

Appendix

Resource A: Sample Menu of Volunteer Positions

In-Person Event

- Setup or load-in
- Teardown or load-out
- Decorating team
- Traffic team
- Information or guest services
- Safety team
- Ushers or greeters

- Room hosts
- Facilities

Virtual Event

- Chat moderators
- Tech support
- Customer service
- Online platform setup/information uploading

At an Organization's Office

- Data entry or administrative support
- Hospitality support
- Receptionist or customer service
- Website editing or updating
- Copywriting or copyediting

Resource B: Sample Position Descriptions

Setup or Load-In

- *Responsibilities*—Meet guest artist's road team and assist with load-in and setup of equipment as directed.

- *Physical Requirements*—Lifting, some over twenty-five pounds, standing, bending, and walking.
- *Expectations*—This position starts very early in the morning.

Decorating Team

- *Responsibilities*—Work with a staff representative beginning eight (8) weeks before the event to assist with brainstorming and designing decor for the event. Arrive to decorate one day prior to the event.
- *Physical Requirements*—Some lifting, standing, sitting, and walking.
- *Expectations*—Must commit to a minimum of five (5) hours per week for eight (8) weeks. Creativity and team collaboration is crucial.

Room Hosts

- *Responsibilities*—Deliver speaker and participant materials to breakout rooms. Greet speaker and keep them on schedule. Welcome attendees and distribute materials as needed. Scan name tags as attendees enter the breakout room.

- *Physical Requirements*—Some standing, sitting, and walking.
- *Expectations*—Must have a welcoming smile and a hospitable personality. These volunteers will be expected to download the event app onto their personal devices for the duration of the event.

Data Entry

- *Responsibilities*—Assist the department with updating its database. Enter attendance after each departmental meeting and transcribe meeting notes.
- *Physical Requirements*—Lots of sitting.
- *Expectations*—Typing skill is a must. Knowledge of the Google Suite of products. Familiarity with transcription equipment is a plus.

Website Maintenance

- *Responsibilities*—Review and update departmental web pages on the organization's website. Create and upload new web page information and images as requested.
- *Physical Requirements*—Lots of sitting.
- *Expectations*—Knowledge of web platforms and functionality required.

Chat Moderators

- *Responsibilities*—Monitor chat feeds as assigned, watch for inappropriate comments, and post references and websites.
- *Physical Requirements*—Lots of sitting.
- *Expectations*—Must have a hospitable personality. Knowledge of virtual events and prior experience with virtual platforms are helpful.

Resource C: Sample Questions for a Volunteer Application

If additional details or clarification are needed, a follow-up phone call is appropriate.

- Are you an introvert or an extrovert?
- Which of these describes you?
  - ○ I am computer savvy.
  - ○ I have organizational skills.
  - ○ I can cook/bake.
  - ○ I participate in sports.
  - ○ I am a handy person.
- Do you prefer to get up early or stay up late?

- How did you hear about this opportunity?
  - Friend or family member
  - Organization's website
  - I received an email.
- Do you have any dietary restrictions?
- Are you allergic to any foods or medications?

Resource D: Sample Table of Contents for a Volunteer Handbook

- About the Organization
  - Mission, Vision, and Values
  - Volunteer Partnership
  - Org Chart
- About the Volunteer Program
  - Overview
  - Structure
  - Expectations
  - Roles and Responsibilities
- About the Event (as applicable)
  - Event Overview
  - Schedule
  - Maps and Emergency Plans

Resource E: Sample Post-Serve Survey Questions

- Did you feel prepared/equipped to perform the tasks you volunteered for?
  - Yes/No
- Did the training materials you receive prepare you to serve?
  - Yes/No
- Was your team leader encouraging and helpful while you served?
  - Yes/No
- Name one thing you would improve about the volunteer program.
  - (Short answer text box)
- Name one thing you appreciated about the volunteer program.
  - (Short answer text box)
- Would you serve on the volunteer team again?
  - Yes/No
- Would you recommend serving on the volunteer team to a friend or family member?
  - Yes/No

Printed in the United States
by Baker & Taylor Publisher Services